THE SKY IS FULL OF SONG

selected by Lee Bennett Hopkins

illustrated by Dirk Zimmer

A Harper Trophy Book

Harper & Row, Publishers

To Sylvia A. Mahler
—a sky-singer
LBH

Acknowledgments appear on pp. 43–45.

The Sky Is Full of Song
Text copyright © 1983 by Lee Bennett Hopkins
Illustrations copyright © 1983 by Dirk Zimmer

Library of Congress Cataloging in Publication Data
Main entry under title:

The sky is full of song.

"A Charlotte Zolotow book."
Summary: An anthology of poems celebrating the
seasons.
    1. Seasons—Juvenile literature. 2. Children's
poetry, American. [1. Seasons—Poetry. 2. American
poetry—Collections] I. Hopkins, Lee Bennett.
II. Zimmer, Dirk, ill.
PS595.S42S5 1983   811'.008'033   82-48263
ISBN 0-06-022582-3
ISBN 0-06-022583-1 (lib. bdg.)

(A Harper Trophy book)
ISBN 0-06-443145-2 (pbk.)

First Harper Trophy edition, 1987

AUTUMN

September

Lucille Clifton

I already know where Africa is
and I already know how to
count to ten and
I went to school every day last year,
why do I have to go again?

Rags

Judith Thurman

The night wind
rips a cloud sheet
into rags,

then rubs, rubs
the October moon
until it shines
like a brass doorknob.

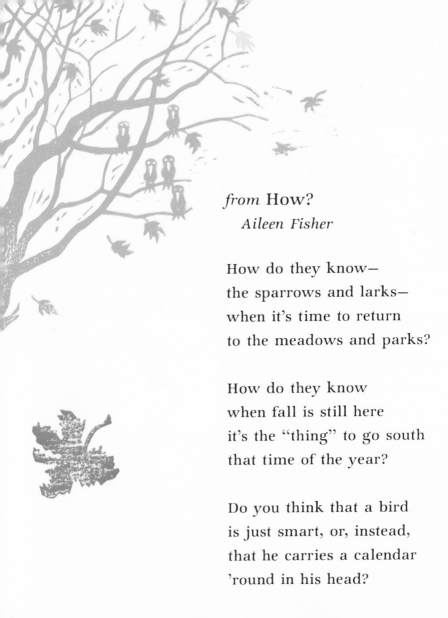

from How?

   Aileen Fisher

How do they know—
the sparrows and larks—
when it's time to return
to the meadows and parks?

How do they know
when fall is still here
it's the "thing" to go south
that time of the year?

Do you think that a bird
is just smart, or, instead,
that he carries a calendar
'round in his head?

This Leaf

Beatrice Schenk de Regniers

This leaf
once
touched
the
sky.
Now it is
dry
crumbs
under my feet.
I
must be
a
Giant.

New Sounds

Lilian Moore

New sounds to
walk on
today—

dry
leaves,
talking
in hoarse
whispers,
under bare trees.

from Witch's Broom Notes
   David McCord

On Halloween, what bothers some
About these witches is, how come
In sailing through the air like bats
They never seem to lose their hats?

The Pumpkin Tide
Richard Brautigan

I saw thousands of pumpkins last night
come floating in on the tide,
bumping up against the rocks and
rolling up on the beaches;
it must be Halloween in the sea.

Thanksgiving

Margaret Hillert

I feel so stuffed inside my skin
And full of little groans,
I know just how the turkey felt
Before it turned to bones.

Fall Wind

Aileen Fisher

Everything is on the run—
willows swishing in the sun,
branches full of dip and sway,
falling leaves that race away,
pine trees tossing on the hill—
nothing's quiet, nothing's still,
all the sky is full of song:
"Winter's coming. Won't be long."

WiNTER

Fair Warning

Norah Smaridge

If you go out without your coat
In damp and chilly breezes,
Your trip will end in BED, my friend,
With fever, chills, and sneezes.

Hungry Morning

Myra Cohn Livingston

In December I remember
In the rain and frosty snow
   hungry cardinals,
   hungry blue jays,
   hungry sparrows: Here I go.

Here's a piece of toast I've saved you
From my breakfast, warm and good,
   hurry cardinals,
   hurry blue jays,
   hurry sparrows: Here's your food.

The Day After Christmas

Lee Bennett Hopkins

The
trash cans
are wrapped
with torn papers
from my presents
and
they wear
a bow
of snow.

December

Sanderson Vanderbilt

A little boy stood on the corner
And shoveled bits of dirty, soggy snow
Into the sewer—
With a jagged piece of tin.

He was helping spring come.

January

Maurice Sendak

In January
it's so nice
while slipping
on the sliding ice
to sip hot chicken soup
with rice.
Sipping once
sipping twice
sipping chicken soup
with rice.

February Twilight
Sara Teasdale

I stood beside a hill
    Smooth with new-laid snow,
A single star looked out
    From the cold evening glow.

There was no other creature
    That saw what I could see—
I stood and watched the evening star
    As long as it watched me.

17

Cynthia in the Snow
Gwendolyn Brooks

It SUSHES.
It hushes
The loudness in the road.
It flitter-twitters,
And laughs away from me.
It laughs a lovely whiteness,
And whitely whirs away,
To be
Some otherwhere,
Still white as milk or shirts.
So beautiful it hurts.

Snowy Benches

Aileen Fisher

Do parks get lonely
in winter, perhaps,
when benches have only
snow on their laps?

Scene

Charlotte Zolotow

Little trees like pencil strokes
black and still
etched forever in my mind
on that snowy hill.

Waiting

Harry Behn

Dreaming of honeycombs to share
With her small cubs, a mother bear
Sleeps in a snug and snowy lair.

Bees in their drowsy, drifted hive
Sip hoarded honey to survive
Until the flowers come alive.

Sleeping beneath the deep snow
Seeds of honeyed flowers know
When it is time to wake and grow.

SPRING

And Suddenly Spring

Margaret Hillert

The winds of March were sleeping.
I hardly felt a thing.
The trees were standing quietly.
It didn't seem like spring.
Then suddenly the winds awoke
And raced across the sky.
They bumped right into April,
Splashing springtime in my eye.

Days That the Wind Takes Over

Karla Kuskin

Days that the wind takes over
Blowing through the gardens
Blowing birds out of the street trees
Blowing cats around corners
Blowing my hair out
Blowing my heart apart
Blowing high in my head
Like the sea sound caught in a shell.
One child put her thin arms around the wind
And they went off together.
Later the wind came back
Alone.

Tommy

Gwendolyn Brooks

I put a seed into the ground
And said, "I'll watch it grow."
I watered it and cared for it
As well as I could know.

One day I walked in my back yard,
And oh, what did I see!
My seed had popped itself right out,
Without consulting me.

April

Lucille Clifton

Rain is good
for washing leaves
and stones and bricks and
even eyes,
and if you hold
your head just so
you can almost see
the tops of skies.

Sidewalk Measles

Barbara M. Hales

I saw the sidewalk catch the measles
When the rain came down today.
It started with a little blotching—
Quickly spread to heavy splotching,
Then as I continued watching
The rain-rash slowly dried away.

The City
David Ignatow

If flowers want to grow
right out of the concrete sidewalk cracks
I'm going to bend down to smell them.

The Shadow Tree

Ilo Orleans

I'd love to sit
　　On the highest branch
But it's much too high
　　For me;

So I sit on the grass
　　Where the shadow falls,
On the top of
　　The shadow tree.

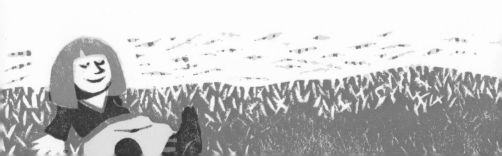

The Merry-Go-Round Horse

Lee Bennett Hopkins

The merry-go-round
    horse has a tear in its eye
left by the spring rain.

May Night

Sara Teasdale

The spring is fresh and fearless
    And every leaf is new,
The world is brimmed with moonlight,
    The lilac brimmed with dew.

Here in the moving shadows
    I catch my breath and sing—
My heart is fresh and fearless
    And over-brimmed with spring.

SUMMER

A Moment in Summer

Charlotte Zolotow

A moment in summer
belongs to me
and one particular
honey bee.
A moment in summer
shimmering clear
making the sky
seem very near,
a moment in summer
belongs to me.

Fourth of July Night

Dorothy Aldis

Just see those pin wheels whirling round
Spitting sparkles on the ground,
And watch that rocket whoosh so high,
Then turn to flowers in the sky—
Green and yellow, blue and red.
And look at ME still not in bed!

Down on My Tummy

Myra Cohn Livingston

I will gather the sunshine in my hands
and lay it warm on the ocean sands
where the sea shells and the waves can see
me, down on my tummy, quietly.

Sitting in the Sand

Karla Kuskin

Sitting in the sand and the sea comes up
So you put your hands together
And you use them like a cup
And you dip them in the water
With a scooping kind of motion
And before the sea goes out again
You have a sip of ocean.

A Year Later
Mary Ann Hoberman

Last summer I couldn't swim at all;
I couldn't even float;
I had to use a rubber tube
Or hang on to a boat;
I had to sit on shore
While everybody swam;
But now it's this summer
And I can!

Crickets

Valerie Worth

Crickets
Talk
In the tall
Grass
All
Late summer
Long.
When
Summer
Is gone,
The dry
Grass
Whispers
Alone.

August Heat

Anonymous

In August, when the days are hot,
I like to find a shady spot,
And hardly move a single bit—
And sit—

      And sit—

           And sit—

               And sit!

August 28
David McCord

A flock of swallows have gone flying south;
The bluejay carries acorns in his mouth.
I don't know where he carries them or why.
I'm never sure I like the bluejay's cry,
But I still like his blue shape in the sky.

Leavetaking

Eve Merriam

Vacation is over;
It's time to depart.
I must leave behind
(although it breaks my heart)

Bullfrogs in the pond,
A can of eels,
A leaky rowboat,
Abandoned car wheels;

For I'm packing only
Necessities:
A month of sunsets
And two apple trees.

Now

Prince Redcloud

Close the barbecue.
Close the sun.
Close the home-run games we won.

Close the picnic.
Close the pool.

Close the summer.

Open school.

Acknowledgments

Every effort has been made to trace the ownership of all copyrighted material and to secure the necessary permissions to reprint these selections. In the event of any question arising as to the use of any material, the editor and the publisher, while expressing regret for any inadvertent error, will be happy to make the necessary correction in future printings. Thanks are due to the following for permission to reprint the copyrighted materials listed below:

Atheneum Publishers, Inc., for "Rags" by Judith Thurman in *Flashlight and Other Poems*. Copyright © 1976 by Judith Thurman. Reprinted with the permission of Atheneum Publishers, Inc.

Clarion Books/Ticknor and Fields, a Houghton Mifflin Company, for "This Leaf" from *A Bunch of Poems and Verses* by Beatrice Schenk de Regniers. Copyright © 1977 by Beatrice Schenk de Regniers. Reprinted by permission of Clarion Books/Ticknor and Fields, a Houghton Mifflin Company.

Curtis Brown, Ltd., for "The Day After Christmas" by Lee Bennett Hopkins. Copyright © 1972 by Lee Bennett Hopkins. "The Merry-Go-Round Horse" by Lee Bennett Hopkins. Copyright © 1976 by Lee Bennett Hopkins. Reprinted by permission of Curtis Brown, Ltd.

Delacorte Press/Seymour Lawrence, for "The Pumpkin Tide" excerpted from *The Pill Versus the Springhill Mine Disaster* by Richard Brautigan. Copyright © 1968 by Richard Brautigan. Reprinted by permission of Delacorte Press/Seymour Lawrence.

Farrar, Straus & Giroux, Inc., for "Crickets" by Valerie Worth from *Small Poems* by Valerie Worth. Copyright © 1972 by Valerie Worth. Reprinted by permission of Farrar, Straus & Giroux, Inc.

Barbara M. Hales, for "Sidewalk Measles." Used by permission of the author, who controls all rights.

Index of Authors and Titles